James Rainsford is the creative pseudonym of K. D. (Brian) Curtis, a writer, photographer and sometime musician. He was raised in Essex, and attended The University of Sussex, where he read Philosophy, English and History. He is married with two children and currently resides in Somerset, UK.

More information is available at: www.jamesrainsford.com

BY THE SAME AUTHOR
Education, Edukation, Edukashun
ISBN 9781905513901

We Cast Pale Shadows

Selected Poems

James Rainsford

Matador
9 Priory Business Park,
Wistow Road, Kibworth Beauchamp,
Leicestershire, LE8 0RX
Tel: 0116 279 2299
Email: books@troubador.co.uk
Web: www.troubador.co.uk/matador
Twitter: @matadorbooks

ISBN 978 183859 260 8

British Library Cataloguing in Publication Data.
A catalogue record for this book is available from the British Library.

Printed and bound in Great Britain by 4edge Limited
Typeset in 11pt Aldine401 BT by Troubador Publishing Ltd, Leicester, UK

Matador is an imprint of Troubador Publishing Ltd

To my parents, who made possible my opportunities to grow and learn how to love and be loved.

To my belovéd wife, Wendy: daughters, Belinda and Debbie, grandchildren, Laura and David and great-grandchildren Olivia and Imogen. They have in their various ways, all been an inspiration. They are my most precious legacy.

Also, to all those teachers, pupils, students, friends, lovers, and especially the beautiful strangers, who knowingly, or unknowingly, have brightened life's journey and made living less a chore and more a rare affair.

I thank them all.

About this poetry collection

The poems selected here for publication were all written over the period from 1964 until 2019. They represent a wide variety of themes and topics and are not organised in chronological or thematic order, but have been selected to illustrate the breadth of interests which have inspired their creation. Randomly interspersed throughout the collection are poems categorised as 'Amuse Bouche,' a phrase borrowed from the restaurant trade and which loosely translates as 'smiling mouth,' they are included to occasionally lighten the mood and provide a contrast to the more contemplative and introspective offerings.

Contents

We Cast Pale Shadows

Déjà Vue

In Memoriam for Betty Hardy

She wasn't you
Standing at an unfamiliar bar
In a Carmarthen pub.
This smiling girl living in your mask
Laughed with another voice.
Surrounded, as you once were
By boys, futureless as memory,
Young as immortality.

No. She wasn't you.
But, only time, and place, and death,
Disproved her face was yours.
And only growing with regret
Kept me from foolishness.
Allowing me to bear the unexpected pain
Of seeing once again, your stunning face
Enthused with life.

No. She wasn't you.
You were three hundred miles
And twenty years away,
And not alive, to hear me say,
I saw your lovely image
Laugh again today.

Fortune

Fortune favours few
who rue the past.
The fast don't last,
the slow go
just the same;
name forgotten.

And although the deal is rotten,
a game where only aces reach
the top
might stop,
unless a common deuce or trey
turns up to make us stay.

A loose deuce can prove worthwhile
and raise a smile.

Remember, most have smiled
when jokers wild, surface
to surprise the smug who hug
a full hand.

For even the lucky lose,
and losers, sometimes win.

Flowers after the Funeral

"And I am dumb to tell the crooked rose"

Dylan Thomas

"Look, we don't love like flowers, with only a single
season behind us;"

Rilke

Flowers lay here,
Dissipating futures
On a dark wind.

Growing; as in our absence
Mountains moved,
Plains settled and grew still.
Enduring chance mutations
Long before aesthetic seasons
Forced their glory
From an ancient breed.
Yet they had need of us,
For it was us
Who gave them name,
Who rearranged each double helix,
Creating fresh displays
Fit for bouquets of death.

We've learned to live,
Aware, all dying wreaths
And we, once shared
The same first stirring
In primeval seas.
Where such potential moved
That we can mould each fading flower,
And are grown mute to tell
Their glory how decay
Shall place our song
Of their short seasons
Against the scale
Which moves the stars.

For, who recalls a poppy
At the gates of Troy,
Or names which garland
Wreathed Achilles' tomb?
What flower loves the seed
From which it came,
Or sees the beauty
In another's bloom?

Guesting in Dreams

When guesting in another's dream
I hope I seem a friendly soul
And play a reassuring role
Dispelling fears so they may reap
The fruits of calm unbroken sleep
And help them wake refreshed, and free
Of care, with thoughts of me
To make them glad I'd brought delight
Into the drama of their night.

Unlike when guests invade my dreams
Bringing landscapes full of dark
Where ghouls and demons bay and bark
Where through some trap-door in my mind
They enter to torment, and bind
My thoughts with chains of fear
That I may not escape from here
Caught forever in their net
Before awaking bathed in sweat.

I wish when guesting in my dreams
The actors would bring peace, not screams.

A Florida Poem

From this far away,
I remember the day
Miami was mine.
The day fine and bright
Was transformed into night
By hotel bars,
Whose gloom tinted the room
To make their welcome warm.
And a car, cool in contrast
To afternoon heat
Ran us down a street
Where nobody walked.

Hey! It was just great
To meet for real the sunshine girls
With come to bed eyes.
It was quite a surprise
To realise, that,
"Have a nice day"
Can be more than just
Something they say
When you pay,
But perhaps their way
Of reflecting the sun,
And implying that fun
Is a possible way

Of making the day
Come alive,
And allowing the night
To arrive with a promise
Of something new,
Where you, or you, or you, and I
Could span the gap
Of culture, time and distance
With an insistence strong enough
To make our feelings real,
And our meeting seem
To make a peal of English Sunday Bells
Sound small and very far away.
So,
"Have a Nice Day",
"You're Welcome!"

Autumn Walk

In almost the last sun of summer
As leaves turn to gold in its light,
We walk towards winter with longing
For lost seasons of earthly delight.

A past when each step had a purpose
And days could endure for years,
We played in our sunshine not knowing
That fevers and time would bring tears.

Now that our seasons are fewer
We've learned to mourn each passing day,
And must live with our future diminished
By time's relentless decay.

Song for an Ex-Wife

Last night,
At the moment between certainty and dream,
The conjuring I had acquired to keep you caged
Was cancelled by a stronger spell.

For even after years,
You came unbidden to my bed,
And tempted love into regret.
Even here; within a bedroom you were
Banished from by my desire,
You found a way to lay
Your ghost beside me,
And possess the still and sleeping form
Of yet another stranger by my side.

When you first left,
To live through our
Shared motion of the sun,
Destroying days with dark mementoes,
And nights with savage wakefulness
Where all alone, I had invoked
The Furies, to pursue your faithlessness
Through every hope you treasured

And held dear
Fear of my wish for your decay
Had marked each day,
With lies to mutual friends,
Who heard I wished you well.

Yet even now;
I burn within the hell
Which I unleashed for you.

Ascent

We have no names
no epic tales cross-checked,
disputed, or distorted
by an antecedent Homer,
so know not for whom, or when
the first flint arced
to scribe the space
between our savagery
and search for explanation
of the stars.

Yet, it was an act
as small as human hand
on fashioned stone which
later was to lay red ochre
on the flanks of beasts
depicted, named and known,
as though creation
waited for this dawn
to show how tools
could grow our wonder
into symbols.

How sureness
in our mastery of stone
would one day
break the sky with spires,
and vault the Earth
with shelter
from the face of god.

As hands taught minds
the certainty which
touch bestowed
we asked first questions
in an extinct tongue.

As muteness waned,
internal spaces grew,
to begin a revelation
which raised Rheims from sand
and sent the sound
of symphonies
to universal ears.

Who first had thoughts to share?
For from this trust
came confidence to tell,
and in the telling
something of the cosmos
was revealed,
shared and made real
by mention of a thought.
As if duration at time zero
deemed it must be thus,
that matter moved, just so
and just so long
as would ensure
that megaliths must be,
and we should mark the passage
of the stars with stones grown
skyward from an instant
in the first event.

In just such seconds as
our physics find too short
for numerals to probe
foundation of our deepest
thought was forged,
as if neutrinos knew
that someday we
would search for them,
and praise creation's scale
with words determined
in the fire which formed
the stars.

Yet, they required us!
It was our amazement
which made praise a
possible event,
and sent sweet music
far beyond the temples
we had built to house our awe.
Without thought no nucleus
would be.
No angel could expect
the supplication of a
bended knee.

Until the double helix
grew, to such complexity,
that we raised questing eyes,
and voiced the long-awaited
'Whys,' which gave the universe a home.

11

Why the waste?
Why so few minds to
give humanity small windows?

Is there not some reason for our doubt?
When faces promise much, and yet
turn in upon themselves
to cancel history with a quip?
Slowing centuries for priests to rule,
or blinding reason with a tyrant's tongue.
Where even Alexandrian sacked
and shattered shelves
could shrink infinity with length.
To leave the last librarian
in fear of Alexander's cowled disciple
paid by us all, to oversee
the infamous destruction of the ending word,
upon the final page,
of the last,
and only book on Earth.

That it shall be,
will rest with the validity
of freedom's claim, to move
beyond the rules, which we devise
to please prediction's need for growth.
Both first and final thought, perhaps,
determined by addition of one zero
in equations no one comprehends.
Who gave the Universe a name
before our early eyes turned skyward?

Who, shall see the death of suns
as but a small event
and after thought is dead
repopulate the heavens
with majestic beasts?

Affair

Christ!
but they're
rare,
The Mondays;
where
A brief affair
can endow
the dawning
of a Tuesday
with a
sense of loss.

Lesson in Falling Over

If you practise falling over
You can become quite skilled.
Avoiding knees grazed,
Elbows skinned.
Of course, when you begin
You must, first place your trust
In one who is prepared
To care enough
To pick the pieces up.

Eventually, you will become
Sufficiently adept, to fall for fun,
Even when attended by
Inept yet trying strangers.
You will however, quickly learn
The danger of
Their slow to catch concern.
And that, if you persist
In going down,
They'll be delighted to
Assist your fall,
With all the force
Their lack of love
Can give the shove
Which puts you down
For good.

Make-up in the Morning

The arched brow receives
Its morning line of painted black.
An eyelash is brushed back in
Concentrated hush, to veil the
Failure of your naked face
To race the blood of strangers
With desire.

The pale lips purse, to meet
The skilful touch of chosen gloss.
Revealing much, of learning skill
To thrill those men with envy
Who cannot possess your masked caress,
Nor leave your bed, with lips
Impressed by red and glazéd
Stain of vain pretence.

This daily ritual of the mask
Becomes a task of no surprise.
I see your peacock eyes express
The lies, which colour hides
From those exposed to self-imposed
Concealment, of the true and
New dawn beauty of your face.

Memory of a Winter Lakeside
at Dawn

Across the chill, still, silent water
of a child's winter lake,
a ghostly iridescent drake,
creates a chevron wake
to break the thin veneer of liquid skin,
and scoops an arc of amber spray,
to catch, the first bright burst
of morning light, that marks night's
sudden death with dawn's revealing rays,
which lays across the shining, sheer
as glass tranquillity of a surface free
from shock, the burning brilliance
of the sun's relentless clock.

Monotheism

Who tends the graves of vanquished gods,
Or fears their ancient powers?
Who carves the dates of their defeat,
Or wreaths their tombs with flowers?

So many deities are dead.
Destroyed by our ungrateful hands
Their proud, yet graven images
Decaying in harsh desert lands.

Each mythic deity displaced,
Once had legions bend the knee
And Vikings prayed that gods would bless
Their raids across a troubled sea.

As one-by-one each god was slain
By converts to the books of death
We lost the chance to grow and bloom
Untroubled by the Devil's breath.

Still three remain, the worst of all
Their cruel demands so widely taught,
Promising eternal fire
For the sin of reasoned thought.

What monster must we now create
To slay these gods of tyranny
Allowing us to dwell in peace
Free from their fearful trinity?

Ascending

Ascending, you shall grow to know
The slow apotheosis of the breath,
Where patient death kindly offsets
The debts you failed to pay.
Vow therefore, from this day
You shall repay the favours shown
For though the end's unknown
It's certain yet.
So leave no stone unturned,
No kindness unreturned.
For thoughtlessness,
Like rampant weeds
Can choke the grandest tomb
With unrequited deeds.

Stone Circle

I'd anticipated more.
More mystery, more magic,
Or, some secret sign to have endured
The silent witness of these standing stones.
Hoping, that some remnant of intention
Had remained;
Revealing early windows
Which Earth's lost light could pierce
To clear my opaque eyes.

Instead, I saw quite clearly
The Neolithic tool marks of the dead,
Their crude labour overscored
With careful carving from a modern hand.

"Sue sucks cocks for 50p

Phone 9573

Cum in the mouth of ecstasy"

And there was me;
My squat thought seeking liberation.

It's a Man's World?

The first thing I need upon waking,
Is a comforting hot cup of tea,
So I turn to my wife to determine
If the maker shall be her; or me.

Sadly, I find her pretending
To be not awake, but asleep,
So I shake her to see if she's faking
And she opens her eyes for a peep.

Then enquires why I have disturbed her,
As she was having a wonderful dream,
So I relate my strong wish for a 'cuppa,'
Which caused an incredulous scream.

Aware that my actions are thoughtless
I give her a kiss and a smile,
So she rises to put on the kettle
And I gratefully sleep for a while.

Upon waking a half-hour later
My tea is as cold as a stone,
My limbs are tied to the bedposts,
But I have the good-sense not to moan.

A Friday Poem

In almost the last sun of summer
a Friday afternoon soon passed.
And time itself seemed fast,
as past and future ceased to be
while we sought to twist eternity
into a shape where we could dwell
untouched by time's decay.

Yet, no day could last the pace.
Your face required more attention
than our time allowed.

The crowd did not exist.
And I missed nothing of your smile,
as lunch-time-halves-of-bitter-men
jostled at the bar.
All were as far away
as possibilities that you,
and I could say enough
to stay the-tick-of-time,
or turn, with all our passionate desire
the coming winter to an instant spring.

And,

time's the thing,
which takes all dreams
and makes all 'seems' the same.

And,

though, I know, the snow will fall
to cover all we shared or had,
I feel so very, very glad
the earth had brought one magic day
To match my thoughts of you,

So new, and yet, so soon to die.

Sonnet to Sanity

This season of the rout of reason
Ripens the toxic fruits of faith,
Infecting guileless children with a love of death.
Blood, stains the hands of zealots
And prompts the lips of leaders to deny the truth
As they try to dissipate our fears with lies.
What are the hopes, of those who value death?
Where are their smiles?
Where their laughter, or their joy
To soften the embrace
Of death's indifference to our love of life?
If tolerance of bad ideas infects the mind
The winding-sheet of death becomes assured,
And all our dreams of life shall be as dust.

A Wasted Week?

Monday was past,
and the rest of the fast
and far-flung week
among the seeking eyes
of other tries
I felt eclipsed.
I thought your lips
were kissed by more
impressive men.
And, I'd felt helpless
to compete with all the neat
and expert tongues,
which sung to you
a sweeter song,
than the one I had rehearsed.

And though my verse
was good enough
for one short night,
even then
the magic of our when
was gently rendered.
Passion surrendered
to the last of separate days
which passed before we met.
Where all my expectations

had yet to be fulfilled
and all my hopes
were stilled by strangeness.
Warning we would part,
before a start was ever truly made.

Eagle

Emblem of lost tribes,
whose chiefs, like envious thieves
had stolen your impressive plumes
to mark their earthbound victories
and swift decaying tombs
with symbols of majestic flight.

With might upon their conquering side
long departed legions, marched beneath
your wings and Rome's green laurel wreath,
bringing death and desperate grief
to stir a new belief, and test opponent's fear
of your talon's deadly strike.

More potent still, was the collective will
of more destructive states.
Whose lust for power, abused your skill
for victory on the wing, to bring new terror
to the tribes of man, misusing your nobility
to glorify their carnivals of death.

Dartmouth

Dreams began here,
Beside tall skyward masts
Whose halyards slap the sound
Of summer's sleepy breeze,
To ease night's humid wakefulness
With the steady tock
Of time's relentless wind,
Which long seasons since had
Sent Crusader's zealous ships
To strange parched landscapes,
Where scorched anxious days,
Chill desert nights, moved
The magic of this place
To repossess the minds of
Men grown weary from
The quest to liberate
Far distant shores,

To have seen those ships
Assembled here!
Knights Templars' golden shields
Bright burnished and reflecting
In an English sun the scarlet
Symbols of the death of God.

This has always been
An estuary of departures,
Leaving long ago to liberate some
Stony ground, grown sterile
From the symmetry of Islam's
Need to scribe and circumscribe
The contours of both lines and lives.

Leaving here requires real reasons.
In any seasons of long years,
Or centuries of slow change
Those who go, would need to know
That absence could rearrange the Earth,
To see the birth of promised lands
Seeded with the hope that something
Of this place, perhaps a trace
Of memory might endure, to summon
Dreams of these steep wooded hills
To illuminate some distant pilgrim's sleep
With reasons to believe in God.

It's hard, even now,
Now that physics has set God to flight,
To see this place and still
Believe that it is all for nought.
That all this beauty, has arisen without thought

If reason leads me to conclude
That standing here on Bayard's Cove
To witness sunset on The Dart
That it, and I, are just an
Accidental part in a cosmic
Game of chance, then I'm just
Pleased, that as time ticks, at least
For me, The Cosmos threw a six.

Angel?

I've seen an angel
disguised in human form
with body warm,
that I am torn
between the expectation
and the salutation due.

And what of you
who merely human are?
Are you so far removed
from all the unrealities of time
that mine,
or her's,
or that's,
or his,
or it's,
or our's
can summon flowers from youth
with tales to teach us truth?

Can our seduction by a bloom
create the room
To feed us space,
To love the face,
To win the race?

You choose,
We lose;
and all the angels everywhere,
despair.

Belonging

As winter encloses us
So too do the restrictions
Of time and place and
Circumstance.

Unlike gods we acknowledge
Our mortality,
And realise our restrictions
Are not home-made,
but
Spring from deeper wells.

Wells, whose walls entrap us
With belonging.
Not to place, or person,
but
To a spring which turned
to flood whilst we were
occupied elsewhere.

And the turbulent tide
Which
Now entraps me,
Tells tales
Which
Takes me from you.

Forgive the water under too many bridges,
Forgive the inability to act,
Forgive the small and subtle
Sequence of events
Which made me thus.

Elegy for a Fox

Displayed behind the public bar
a small, now silent fox's head
casts its final blind and mindless stare
across the room,
where a careless crowd of rowdy men,
cheerfully ignore the fact,
that its tired and tarnished plaque,
proclaims a small, sad,
act of a once country sport.

Compared to the concerns of greater kills,
it's no surprise that this,
its last and sightless gaze
should fail to amaze, or, move our
proven need to seed the air
with failure on a larger scale.

And why; among them all,
should its panting tongue
be sung a dirgeful song?
When all the wrong we've done
to each, and everyone,
can teach us to reserve
our highest curve of grief
for the relief of human death.
Where breath has been extinguished

on more distinguished fields,
than those, where hunted foxes
lose the final chase.

In secret places, where
the bloody brush is smeared
on young flushed cheeks,
which future joys of innocence
shall send a blush of coyness,
that will mask the tainted,
painted skin,
that hides within the tender face
the sublimating carnal race,
and their meagre fall from grace.

Our belief that the demise
of one small and scruffy thief
merits no surprise, and prompts
no whys of conscience to disturb
the placid path of easy laughter.
The fox's death is understood,
against the scale,
which needs the ill of greater deeds
to feed the will to action.

But, after all the tall and
bright-eyed-bushy-tales are told,
we still unfold the tragic fact
that whilst we can accommodate
the common fate of one small
and furry pest, then, crest its
tiny severed head, with deadly pride
beside forgetful fruits for all to see,
we shall not mend the mind
which finds exhilaration
in annihilation of a nation-state.

The same force, which seeks
a source of joy from the safety
of the ritual death of one small life,
can plunge the knife into a thousand guts.
Or, stand aside, and watch the tide of blood;
flood from the cuts
which bleed humanity to death.

Enlightenment

Whilst black holes in space can pull stars to oblivion,
And physicists dream in their own special idiom
Of macro and micro, or quasars and quarks,
You might be forgiven for feeling this marks
The end of a story, which finally brings,
A beautiful unification to things.

Yet beyond our desire to comprehend stars
Or, send Earth's ambassadors winging to Mars,
We need to confront the cults of conviction,
So keen to embrace the dangerous fiction
That their loving god is clearly so great,
He fills his believers with murderous hate.

For a Friend Buried at Saint Mary's Churchyard Hawkesbury

25th November 1980

Spring has arrived here again;
Growing his colours across
The quilted countries of your truth,
Finding in each waxing moment
Fresh fertility, to form anew
The atlas of familiar fields.
Fields, where you had grown,
Enduring many seasons of his pulse.
Learning as you grew,
That even here, where in the mist
Of last November's thin grey rain
We left your winter mound unmade
He would return; to conjure
From your fading flesh
The irony of birth.

Growing from your final bed
The transmuted beauty
Of posthumous flowers.

Self-Censorship

Not to offend we
bend and twist
all that we say,
in case we might convey
a prejudice, which
tragically may prove,
we strongly disapprove
of being killed
for questioning
the certainty of faith.
We need to learn,
not all beliefs
are worthy of respect
not all views are equal
when compared.
And though we're scared,
we must confront
those who desire
to cast our freedoms
into the fire
of their imagined hell.

September Meeting

For Mary, who restored my sight.

It was you,
stranger in a strange land;
possessed with eyes blue as hyacinths,
innocent as birth,
blameless as death's cold love
for all our brief imaginings.
You! who called from hibernation
all those great and sad perspectives
sharp with joy and desolation.
You! who faced me with such instant love,
that I, caught in the slowness
of low expectation,
almost failed to perceive
how in your voice "forever" breathed.
And through your life lost kingdoms moved,
and were restored for me.

That you should be the catalyst for this.
The last great journey of the mind,
where separation from the sound
of solar wind was healed.
Where I became the stuff of stars,
and knew myself to be at home
in strange unconscious streets, whose

temporal testament to many gods
flowed stony through my blood.
That you, though unaware, should
see the supernova of the heart's
last true and guileless grief,
to leave a pulsar at my soul
so black, that life itself
is captive at my core.

That I should be made whole
for just one moment by your touch,
and meet again the Angel of the Elegies,
who at Duino had vouchsafed
a vision to a fellow mind
which would have understood
how through your eyes
infinity surprised my soul,
and startled me from sleep.

Wise Blood

A Prayer for Hazel Motes

Place him in the sun,
Where scorched sands
Deny most trying beasts a home,
Where light will leave him sightless
In the white day,
And night shall bring such chill
That pale stars
Will burn his eyeless skull.

Leave him to learn
The strange economy of lizards,
And pray with me,
That he shall come to know
That sometimes;
Gods destroy us in capricious ways.

Autumn Express

Racing to horizons where the rails
Appear to meet, but never do,
Travelling forever, side-by-side,
Both leading to the end,
Both linked and needed
But not joined as one.
The journey has begun,
Late autumn sun
Crimson like the last leaves
Lingering on frosty boughs
Lights the backs of houses
As we depart the town.
Trapped behind the carriage-glass
The landscapes pass,
Ephemeral as a movie frame
Each fleeting scene
A dream of 'might have been,'
Where other lives are lived
In unfamiliar streets.
No stops now
Before the final destination.
Station after station
Pass into history
As passengers recede
Into the past

Like ghosts awaiting
Their own journeys
To the last stop on the line.
And for us all
The terminus awaits,
End of the track.
In front the buffers
Stop our journey hence.
Behind, the guard,
His signal now at red,
Ensures we can't return.

The verb/adverb way to start the day!

Wake gradually,
Yawn luxuriously,
Sigh sleepily,
Stretch languidly,
Scratch contentedly,
Touch tenderly,
Caress lovingly,
Persuade coaxingly,
Kiss erotically,
Swell manfully,
Rise hurriedly,
Apologise profusely,
Leave quickly,
Piss ecstatically,
Shake vigorously,
Fart quietly,
Return sheepishly,
Speak flatteringly,
Resume eagerly,
Lick lasciviously,
Rub unceasingly,
Harden perceptibly,

Lubricate discretely,
Enter slowly,
Slide gently,
Build consistently,
Move arousingly,
Whisper obscenely,
Listen attentively,
Thrust furiously,
Moan convincingly,
Climax noisily,
Come copiously,
Subside sensuously,
Withdraw carefully,
Wipe thoroughly,
Compliment sincerely,
Thank gratefully,
Look adoringly,
Smile smugly,
Depart regretfully.

Separation

Tonight a candle consumed itself in vain.

For in this plush, lush atmosphere
Of soft lights and music sweet,
It's just to eat
I sit and wait.
And;
A half-empty plate
Is my view.
Instead of you,
I must make do
With waiters who,
Though willing,
Perform to a lone audience of one,
Instead of two.

And where are you?
You; who
Are required to lend significance
To this occasion where,
A bare
Place and empty chair,
Prepare me for the loneliness to come.

I'd like to know,
That even though
We are apart,
That for you too,
There is a space unfilled.

Tonight a candle consumed itself in vain,
Burning fiercely with the pain
Of separation.

She Was

She was pregnant,
She's been rolled,
She was ugly,
She's too bold,
She was scruffy,
She's so cold,
She was stupid,
She's too old,
She was crazy,
She's been sold.

I just wish
That I'd been told
They broke the mould
Where angels grow
So very, very, long ago.

Where is the Child?

Where is the child
Who has moved through thirty winters
Since he watched his father
Try to bowl a cricket ball?
And who, by careful coaching elsewhere,
Understood, that the action of the arm was wrong,
Scribing through the child's unblemished run
Of seven faultless summers, a clumsy arc,
Which sent the ball too wide
And called from restless slumber
A spectre of uncertain shape and size.

Where is the child
Who saw his father's failure
Force derision from each watchers eye
And shared their scorn, yet was ashamed.

Where is the child
Who learned too fast
The legacy of adoration,
And impotently sent imaginings
From fevered nights to boil
Each mocking eye in blood.

Where is the child
Who felt confusion; anger,
Then, the dormant seed of virulent contempt
Germinate, strike root, grow, bud and bloom,
Finding instantly, a fallow vein
In which to flower for his father's sake.

Where is the child?
Where is the child now?

His desolation lives between these lines.
His uncomprehending eyes plead from every word,
At each full stop he mutely tries to speak.

Just once, his hand stretched from this page
To touch my own.

Songs and Seasons

Songs and seasons separate our souls.
Long before our different roles
Can be fondly intertwined,
Or, we can find some common ground
To plant our love in fertile soil.
It's easy for us both to spoil
The promise of our hopeful start
With vain wishes, which
Will drive our dreams apart.
Come listen to my grieving heart
Which traces time's indifference
To our deepest needs,
And feeds our isolation
With sad songs of separation.

Saloon Bar Super Heroes

A tribute to the devotees of
Space Invaders

It's not just imagination
that minds throughout the nation,
have been subtly invaded
by machines which have persuaded,
even reasonable men,
that a few pounds worth of pleasure
can provide the kind of leisure,
which presents them with a challenge
to their skill.

This second generation of micro-chip-elation
are seducing fools,
producing rules
of inane concentration and total fascination;
reducing all who pay and play
to sad saloon bar starship captains
whose pyrrhic scores in phoney wars
cause insane wins to light up grins,
revealing joys in tempting toys
of futile fights.

Every night they dice with fate
and sublimate the will to hate
in raucous celebration of their own annihilation
by bouncing beams which in my dreams
engenders screams for silence.

If any aliens are waiting,
and at this moment contemplating,
contact with the denizens of earth;
then I think it's worth their noting
that the games we are promoting,
were not worth a trip of light-years to observe.

What Dream is This?

What dream is this?
That you and I
may kiss tonight?

A temptress from afar
has placed starlight
in your eyes,
and its twinkling
brightness just belies
the sighs and cries and whys,
which will surely follow this.
Our first, exploratory kiss.

The Bell Ringers

"Never send to know for whom
the bell tolls; it tolls for thee."
John Donne: 1572-1631

From ancient towers
Generations of departed hands
Have rung the knell
Of passing ghosts.
Sounding 'dings'
And dirgeful 'dongs.'
Sending soulful songs
Down lost Sundays
Of the dead,
Instilling dread.
The chilling figure's
Keenly sharpened scythe
Nearer with each chime.
As time takes his toll.
Each dying soul
Adds to the growing roll-call
Of the dead.
Inside my head
A distant bell
Begins to also ring,
Marking the tiny 'ding'
Of my short life
Against the scale
Of distant stars.

"And builds A Hell in Heaven's Despite"

To William Blake

Together in your high dome
The lamb and the dream of death,
dwelt,
irreconcilable.

Your eternal forehead,
Where the visions heat was
burned
in
pain
Showed us the world.
The Hands,
The Christ,
The God,
The DEATH.

You left us a dream,
and
a rose we can't cure.

Traveller

I stood, silent, looking back
Along the sometimes rutted track
I'd travelled from the start.
Its source, long since obscured
By wandering ways
And lived-in-days
Prevented me from seeing
That this day would come,
When I should stand amazed
At the variety of ways
Which faced me now.

On the journey here
I'd passed side streets
But, fear had kept me
On the narrow path which
Marked the progress of my past
With pace too fast for pause,
With step too sure for exploration
Of potentially exciting;
Certainly inviting
Roads of possible reward.

I was not lead astray
To tread diversions posted by the weak.
Nor did I once turn back,
To seek the sheltering safety
Of a friendly cul-de-sac.

Forward, always forward
Seemed the sensible response.
Resisting tempting lanes of futures missed,
The scarcely kissed and grieving girls
Left lonely, at the stations of sensations
Long abandoned on a dusty trail
Which stretches back as far as mind
Can find a tale to tell.

And yet, it all seemed well enough.
The occasionally tough and taxing hills
Were soon forgotten in the compensating thrills
Of easy down-hill-rides,
And, until now the route's been nice,
The fruits of paradise, not hard to find.
The journey's time, mostly remembered
As a swiftly winding walk of pleasant talk
With tardy friends, who, far behind
Still wend their way, with time of day
To stop and say "hello!" to slower men.

How could I know the road would cease to be?
I had no map, and could not see this far.
I did not know this star of future streets
Greets all who run the race on single tracks.

Turning, I look forward.

In front of me, I see
A meeting-of-the-ways, so vast,
That everywhere I cast my eyes
A hundred long and lonely highways,
Bursting like the first rays
Of a newly risen sun
Surround me
And, confound me
With the question
Of which one to choose.

To lose my chosen path this late.

Capricious fate has frozen action here.
The barren landscape's mute,
No clue to future route.

I stand, alone at last.

Amidst an enigmatic land
The past, a stream of shrouded sand
Which trickles through the ageing fingers
Of my wasted hand, has closed her gate

And, though I wait,
I know I can't remain.
The painful choice of many roads
Determined by a view imposed
So long ago, disdains to show the way.
This day's decline has found the time
To prove pervasive darkness mine.

There's no retreat,
A fleeting glance all time's allowed
Before the fruitless furrow ploughed
Is veiled with hastening weeds.
Whilst, future seeds are being sown
To germinate in soil unknown.

The day descends, darkness ascends.

As I shake free the tyranny
Of turnings past, to slowly take
The first awakening step in fading light,
Uncertain stars of clear and curving night
Illuminate my right to choose.

Pray God! I shall not lose again.

Twilight Meetings

The busy person's crazy
alternative to breakfast
meetings

Any illuminating beams, these insanely timed,
Yet evocatively entitled gatherings
May shine upon life's problems,
Are inevitably dimmed
By the lack of light
Emanating from
Those
Who, easily coerced,
Stupidly attend!

Literary Critic

On TV, a critic
exclaimed with conviction,
he could never accept
a poetic fiction,
which included as part
of the verse makers art
the word "proceeding".
He thought it was leading
to a too legal reading
of words meant
to inspire not tire.

The PC pallets of literary lice,
can sometimes entice
a poet of promise
to sadly forget,
the whole of language
is caught in his net.

And that,
the freedom to choose
the words he may use;
is his own.

This Year's Deaths

Many dreams ago, love was manifest, but now
there's nothing more of which we
can sing.

The birds have long since left, and in their
place has come the winter, and though I have
endured past seasons, this year something has
died in me too.

I also yearned for the miracle, when hair like
horses manes would defy the breeze of summer.
When eyes like burning suns would see my soul,
see: and know I was desperate too.

Love me for the reasons that I once found
within myself, and now no longer feel.
Give me my life that once again I may wake
to hear birds sing, and in the coming spring
see them make their nests from this year's deaths.

Venus in a Public Bar

So beautiful that time slowed to silence,
She moved through memories,
Disturbing dominoes, reviving dreams.
Inciting whispers and wistful
Glances from old men,
Who regretfully remembered,
When such beauties as they'd known
Still had long lives ahead
And hopeful futures in an antique bed.

Food Festival

Overnight the town has changed
With streets and car parks rearranged,
Marquees blossom to become
Tarpaulin temples to the tum,
Where stalls arise equipped to feed
This new gastronomy of greed.

Here there are cheeses, and chocolates and jams
Chillies and juices, beef-jerky and hams.
Wines, beer and meats and colourful jellies
All destined for mouths and very fat bellies
Which wobble and bobble from breakfast to dinner,
Each owner bemused as to why they're not thinner.

By noon the marquees are full to capacity
With visitors lost in voracious rapacity.
Chomping and swigging on taste-bud temptations
Offered by vendors from far-away nations.
They queue at the hog-roast awaiting their turn,
Consuming more calories than they'll ever burn.
Blaming their waistlines upon sluggish glands
As their very large frame forever expands.

See photographers roam with long lenses extended,
To shoot famous chefs who've proudly attended
To recreate all of their signature dishes,
From exotic veg and very strange fishes.
Surrounded by groupies with newly bought books
Written by precious overpaid cooks.
Hoping that once the demo is through
They'll be able to wangle a selfie or two.

Outside of the tents musicians enact
Music and dancing to try and distract
An audience keen to return to the fray
Of eating and drinking and chewing their way
Through all of the 'goodies' still to be bought,
Before stalls are depleted and offering nought.

As darkness descends at the end of the day
Most sated gluttons are drifting away.
Some to seek solace in a food-friendly pub
Where they can consume yet more tasty grub,
While others head home to their fifty-inch tellies
Complaining about their gaseous bellies.

The young post their selfies and comments on twitter.
While locals are left to clear up the litter.
Finally free of this greedy occasion,
Yet dreading the next gastronomic invasion.

Devon Sunset

Trees' tortured forms
Crackle through the scarlet
Of departing day with
Shapes sinister and strange.
Ascending like black lightning.
Seeking succour from the
Blood of light's farewell.
Leaving legacies to beauty,
And bequeathing to the chill
Of an uncertain night
The vision of a burning sky,
A stunning tribute to the
Sun's incredible goodbye.

What About Now?

What about now?
Must we wait until love dies?
Or, can we lasso light and
Capture in our fragile arms
The joy which sunshine brings,
Leaving loss to wither
On dead boughs
Like last year's fallen
And forgotten leaves
Transforming lives forever?

The death of decaying seasons
Forever fades, bringing once again
The majesty of spring,
Where you and I, can tenderly
Bear witness to the frailty of love.

Some People I Know

Some people I know
have failed to grow.
Others sprout poison like weeds.
Still more root in gravel,
or travel like seeds
blown by winds and
bending like reeds.
Some whom I've loved
have shrivelled and died,
been cast upon compost,
or broadcast so wide
their memory fades
like the flowers of spring.
Whilst the best have blossomed
to make my heart sing.

It's such a shame
when those we can tame,
remain forever,
exactly the same.

Any Dream

Any dream of might have been
destroys a scene
faster than a fork of lightening
fells an oak,
which reared a thousand years,
and wept no tears,
in growing, or in going.

For some, a tree
may be no more than wood.
Which could have been by-passed
but for its lasting value to
the few who fell the trees
to profit from a landscape
left with silence.

Mark well that birds have gone,
and where their song
once echoed through
the green,
the scene
is stark
the prospect dark,
and people,

more fruitless
than the forests,
here take root.
Possessed of static seasons
their expectations are all of winter.
A splinter from their touch
would kill dreams faster
than it takes the last
and tallest tree to fall
to leave us all in landscapes
lost in dust.

For in the face of futures
which depend on what has been,
a dream or two can go astray,
but if none stay,
we're dead,
long, long
before the final bed, is made.

Armistice Day

Field days of hypocritical sadness,
are,
represented by,
Rows of dejected heads,
and
many wrinkled eye-lids
which should hide self
blaming tears of grief.

Heads in ceremonious lines,
and,
eyes too worn from seeing
peer
almost sightlessly across
November wind to
where bronze discs
on dirgeful breasts
hang,
for services rendered.

And,
in the obelisk shadow of dead names,
are
laid the tokens of yearly conscience
which we call respect.

The End Begins

The end begins,
not with the first stain
of red sputum on a white handkerchief.
Nor by fingers grown numb with
seizure from the heart's decay.
But, with an act
that leaves a toy discarded
in the nursery of early choice,
reviving for abandoned deeds
the doppelgängers of dead youths,
clothed with reproach and unfleshed
figments of the mind's high hopes of
futures fenced in a child's green field
that now is hedged; and ploughed,
and grown bitter with a
named and known crop.

The Intensely Loved

The intensely loved and cherished child,
Can suffer late.
Waiting; innocently through,
The too few summers
Spent in total love.

Above him still; the parents' strength,
Prescribes the length
His loving years shall run,
Before time's taint reveals his ancient face
Beneath the slowly peeling paint
Of pictures placed
To keep the knowing day at bay.
And stay completion of the plan
To mould the clay in such a way
He grows, a sold and silent man.

Unless; time slays his shining sun.
To extinguish all sensation
In one swift and savage stroke,
Before a doubt is spoken,
Or disaffection's woken
From his learning touch.

He, perhaps, expects too much.
Such is the faith of infants
Safe within the fragile skin,
So thinly wrought in thoughtful art,
That, heart's wild wishes can depart
But, disenchantment can't see in.

When the World Was

When the world was wish full
there were walks which
always lead somewhere.

Going and coming back
was not as now
a circular event,
with forced purpose but no point.
Each step extended boundaries,
and the world
was still small-windowed
by the first frontiers.

The Kind of Care I Care About

I'd admit to a prejudice,
But, banality is too widespread
To prove the dead live only here.

I've moved, year after year.

Wearied by the search for fonder minds
The finds I make tend for the sake of self.
Take, not give, the living way.
Pay, and don't stay to hear unsubtle stories,
Trivial glories given status undeserved.

I'd like to say that other's gifts
Were lifted without payment.
But, the price I pay for sanity
Confirms the pity of a culture
Which can lure ten million minds
To live within the score of finds
Reduced by mass-produced response.

Aware;
The kind of care I care about
Is touted by the few,
I must make do with plundering
The wonder of remembered views,
Where time and place were peopled
By a different race than these,
Who learn so early how to turn
Such slight concerns into a view
Which does not grow.
Consigns expectancy to youth
And sheds the truth too soon
To leave sufficient room
For all the womb bred promise
Of the hopefulness of youth

Allowing us to die
Knowing that the truth
Is rarely told, and our compassion
Makes us slaves, to emotions
That are bought, and sold by knaves.

Final Silence

there are no birds,
or flowers,
or running
hand in hand.

hopeful eyes,
once mirrored
in imagined futures
reach their final view.

parched lips,
upon whose
cracking flesh
wine flowed,
laughter bubbled,
and love pressed
his brief desire
now fade.

lined hands,
once moved with gestures
touched by dreams,
claw the winding shroud
with talons of despair.

I care,
for everyone who
dies,
not knowing
where the time has gone,
or why.

we die
no closer to the truth,
yet having known the
intense fragility
of our ephemeral youth.

The Wasteland Revisited

T.S.E. and I may disagree
That April supreme possesses
The power that caresses
The life from infertile earth.

The worth of a season
In prompting a reason
For passion or care
Is not the affair
Of April alone.
For seeds which were sown
Aeons ago,
Can produce in the snow
A dream that will throw
Through the stoniest ground
A growth;
Whose sound alone could shake the stars
And make gods quake in fear,
At what,
Perhaps mistakenly,
They have created here.

A Sonnet to Natasha

I took your thoughts to bed tonight.
Though we have never met,
nor maybe ever will.
Still, I shared your verse with her I love.
Softly breathing dreams beneath the same
celestial sphere, which cover you and us
from where you are, to here.
Your words, created far away,
touched our fragile lives today.
And though our years and lives
and loves are continents apart,
something of your poet's soul
has journeyed here, and
moved our mutual heart.

To Ernie, who used to play dominoes at my local pub

Finally, done with raw ambition,
Drink, dominoes and conversation
Now acquire their always
More important role.

Done with tedious time encroaching tasks
The truth now takes all lunchtime in its telling,
And requires a round or two of bitter beer
To bring the pains and pleasures
Of a poignant past
To the point of purpose.

And as I sit and play,
And pay to learn,
It's more than debts and dots and dominoes
For which I spend.

I listen to the splendours of past springs,
Which make sense of this, my present summer.

I travel with the tales which traverse time,
And take comfort from the continuity which
Turns around this tavern table.

For the tales and their telling
Makes time terminal,
And all the terrors of a transitory life
Become bequeathed.

Such bequests, remind me what has been,
Enable me to live with that which is,
And nurture me to bear what may become.

We'll know this Love

A Villanelle for Wendy

We'll know this love until our last goodbyes,
Till on my grave is laid your last bouquet,
Until no tears shall moisten these blind eyes.

Though we may never understand the 'whys,'
Our love will mark the minutes of each day,
We'll know this love until our last goodbyes.

We've glimpsed the lows, aspiring to the highs,
We'll move in sunlight though the sky is grey,
Until no tears shall moisten these blind eyes

If death's the end, then love is the surprise,
That's proven life is more than a cliché,
We'll know this love until our last goodbyes.

Throughout the minutes till my final cries,
I'll treasure all you do, and all you say,
Until no tears shall moisten these blind eyes.

For sharing love has been our greatest prize,
All of life's pain its presence can outweigh,
We'll know this love until our last goodbyes.
Until no tears shall moisten these blind eyes.

Time and Seasons

Time and seasons take high tolls,
Unweaving links which bind young souls.
Neglected steps foretell the end
Too steep to climb, too late to mend.
Once planted deep in fertile ground
Love's tendrils have become unwound.
Filling spaces with regret
Recalling times love can't forget,
Lamenting life's sad isolation
Seeking songs of separation.

To my daughter for a day
remembered

My three-year-old daughter
Bubbling with laughter
Sang to me a sweet song
In a long-ago summer.

Fresh washed and brushed blond hair,
A pair, of bright white shoes
Gave this girl in new blue dress
And eagerness for lucid life
A twirling grace, that framed the
Face with swirling curls, which spoke
Of innocence to win the race
By perfect form and fortune born
Of pure and guiltless mind.

Remind me; despite my tender care,
That this fair and loving child
Was an embryonic wild, and wanton woman;
Whose finite measured days of fun
The sun disdainfully allowed to run;
Whilst guileless beauty, golden, turning,
Passed the infant hours of learning
Unaware that time had planned
A moving of the hour hand

To end the promise
Of this fresh-faced start
In pain the coming rain would surely bring,
Filling the learning years with knowing tears
To slowly stain this new and true blessed heart,

And force; this singer, and her song,
A long; long way apart.

Who Will?

How many thoughts depart
each time a mind goes out?
How many brilliant, or dull dreams,
does death disperse?

Who will wonder why
when we're *all* gone?

Where's Wordsworth?

This morning William,
trees in spring splendour
endeavoured to impress me.

Birds sang, and in their voice
no sour note was struck
to soil the serenity
of these signifiers of spring.
Signs and symbols of Earth's ripeness
wrapped me in their siren song
of a season plump with promise.
Significance danced in sunbeams
and poets posturing prior to me
before these portends passed,
and added to the morning's call
their long-departed pastoral dream
that we are one with all things green.

But, existing now,
not in some lost idyll
I'm disenchanted by the
pledge of daybreak.

For a decade of delightful dawns
induces numbness,
and all the efforts of the earth
in bloom are not enough to block
the boredom of this
morning's birth.

A New Face

We'd only just met,
and yet, I had a premonition
that fruition would fulfil the promise
of this still and silent space
with future faces lip-to-lip.
And that together we should sip
a draught from deeper streams
than these small seems
of one day dreams,
which filled our eyes
and stilled our whys of when,
to wait a later date,
where fate had laid aside sufficient time
to turn this mime of first desire
into a fire fierce enough to burn away the fears,
and hot enough to melt the years of separation.
Proving to us both, 'Elation Lives'
And gives to those, who dare to pose the question
A rarity of find that mind alone can't comprehend.

Perhaps I'm wrong; and we shall not meet again,
If that proves true, at least this song's for you.
And you are due this token,
For having woken feelings which I feared had fled,
And showing me, that even when the expectation's dead
A look was shared, surprising eyes which cared,
And cherished hopes I thought had perished
with the truth, that only youth seemed heir to.

Childhood and Dunkirk

A seven-year-old boy lay prone on a carpet of green,
Sown with care to cover the nakedness of soil.

How well the innocent

Apes the dead who laid on a crimson cloth
Woven with torment, to cover the nakedness of sand.

While the little one lay feigning death
I watched him.

The life-blood etched upon his temple,
Spoke of frailty.

Words

Words, words, words, words,
Used by sages, used by fools,
Used by those who write the rules.
Used to flatter and deceive,
Used to make the poor believe
That heaven is their just reward,
That death upon the victor's sword,
That butchery in holy wars
Is dying in a noble cause.

Words, words, words, words,
Used to chide and used to praise,
Used to wound and to amaze,
Used to seduce and to persuade,
Used to make the weak afraid,
To mould their minds and control
The fate of their immortal soul.
To command them, and ensure
Obedience to the rule of law.

Words, words, words, words,
Used by beggars and by kings,
Used to give ideas new wings,
Used to comfort and cajole,
Used to act the tyrant's role,
So all conform to power's need
To feed the unremitting greed
Of those contemptuous of the poor,
Forever taking more and more.

Words, words, words, words,
Used by the young and by the old,
Used to fashion and to mould.
Used by warriors and priests,
Used to calm life's savage beasts
So we can sleep through fearful nights
Dispelling ghosts with words of light
Connecting us with other minds
Where we may make the greatest finds.

Words, words, words, words,
Used to condemn and to forgive,
Used to say who dies, and who may live,
Used to teach and used to learn,
Used to say who'll crash and burn.
Yet, the finest use I know,
Is when words are used to show
We value friends, and that above,
All things on earth, we value love.

Zenith

To Martin in Memoriam

There was a moment when you seemed to reach perfection.
When expression, word, gesture, touch, look, understanding,
demeanour and desire coalesced, creating for your friends,
an envelope of hope.

Such wholeness can't endure.
Nor could we witness, or preserve its force
with wobbly words.

But, even though the moment, like you,
has passed beyond recall,
One friend at least, remembers when
Your presence altered space, slowed time,
bent sunbeams, so we moved in light.

Divorce

One thought possesses me.
Did you dream this end?
And if you did,
Is all our laughter cancelled?
Are our shared moments of glad grace
Devalued by this last event?
And if they are,
How can we conjure hope
To buttress frail desire
That love could come again,
Clothed in uncertain dreams
And not lasciviously draped
With this savage livery of loss?

Revolution

Has now the season for the death of reason come?
Will all the scared, prepared to run
Wish to partake the death of sanity,
And cloud the sun with poison from a billion minds?

The signs are here to see,
How even brave men flee the realms of reason,
To rage and hate and kill and burn.
Can we expect to learn in time
The way to turn the passing passion
To a rational response?

Have we collectively, not challenges enough
To tempt the tough to actions?
Without the need to feed the fetid fears
Of frightened men with worries when the blow will fall.

For I fear the factions
Whose rule has reason-on-the-run.

The call to chaos is a loss to all mankind
And, we shall not find solutions in the resolutions
From the rulers of unstable suns,
Nor will fanatics find that minds expand in desert sand,
Where a spasm of enthusiasm rekindles old ideas,
And could create sufficient hate
To sacrifice the price of thought,
And leave us with the nought
Which ought to make us cease.

The price of peace may be too high,
But, its value fills the sky with greenness
Which the fury of the desert dust denies.

And leaves the earth
To seek rebirth from cosmic sighs,
Which propagate the lies
Upon the lonely breath of uninvited death.

Tomorrow's Country

When the future
could imagine me,
all its promise,
projected
possibilities
unending.

Then I laughed
among its moment
measured years.
A place in time
where swallows stayed
all winter watching,
as spring unwound
to stop at
summer.

Now my summer's
finite.
The spring unwinds
accelerating time.
Tracing on the face
of season after season
the fading green of
fullness unfulfilled.

Must every journey
to tomorrow's country
bring with it now
this certainty of sameness?

Will every future
have to be imagined?
And in the act
will all its promise
turn to dust?

The Women who Amaze me Most

_____

The women who amaze me most
are those, who boast a body
close to perfect.
Then, elect to dress in less
than is required to prevent
my tired eyes from rising
to observe the tantalizing curve
of well-filled blouse, or
arouse my baser feelings
with revealing sight
of tight split skirt,
exposing, toes to thighs
a glimpse of leg which begs
my chance unhurried glance
to pause, and cause reaction.

But, the action which they take
to quickly make some small
and fake adjustment to their dress
reveals the sweet distress
my eyes caress has caused.

They are aware, their choice attire
has stirred desire, and yet react
with tactile skill to close the split
which tempted it to surface.

I'd love to kill their expectation
for a thrill-inducing chance
to show their slow, deliberate disapproval
of my supposed unwelcome glance.

Yet, just like less self-conscious men
I find myself ensnared again,
to render satisfaction to their skilled
and ancient action, to elicit a response
they can wantonly reprove
with one smooth and practiced
movement of a hem.

The Invitation

I invite you to
A change of view.
Where you and
I
May witness day,
A time to play,
Before we also
Die.

To Personify

Once upon a time
There were two,
Him and I,
He being LIVE
And I being DIE.

He had gone out
For a walk
In the snow,
His eyes alight
His face aglow.

I followed him down
To the edge
Of the sea;
There all alone
Just him, just me.

When he reached the point
Where the sea
Met the snow,
He turned and said
"Come, let us go."

I looked around slowly,
Scanned the beach
And the sea,
No one was there
He was talking to me.

So I gave him my hand,
He grasped it
With laughter,
And pulled me headlong
Into the water.

Now I am alone,
You see
I can swim,
He had given me back
What I'd given to him.

Even Now

Even now,
the fascination of the faith compels.
But, how to tear oneself away?

The way began amid the myths
simplified to suit the kids
supplied with only simple dreams.
And, for a while
the well-intentioned smile
of a Calvinistic style,
impressed us to be good,
and do what must be done,
to provide us with the billionth
part of sunshine which God decreed
was all we needed to survive.

Alive? We've managed that.

All we'll require to keep their fires burning,
or; in turning, all the energy we'll ever need
to feed the coming cries of newborn 'whys'
to perpetuate the fate of all the small
and silent men, who've no idea if, or when
their day will dawn.

To spawn for centuries
the children of small comfort,
and, deliver their tall thought
into the bought and tainted hands
of panders to negation, that
the Reformation profits brought.

The child's caught desires,
sometimes can refute
the profitable pyres.
Purchased by suppression
of his growing pain.
Which darkly dwells
within the cells,
of his quick and able brain.

Again, and yet again,
the story's told,
to unfold 'Creation's Myth' to children,
when all they can achieve,
is leave the gift of toil,
lest their aspirations spoil
the red and fertile soil
which favours few with fortunes.
And opportunes the rest, and rarely blest
to fester; angry in a future sold
by spinners of the most,
corrupting story ever told.

I
_____

Fragmentary pieces now are all that's left of
two
who
Laid their careful footsteps side by plastic
side
Across the summers m
e
l
t
i
n
g Earth.

II
_____

Keep walking,
till
the soul shall
kiss
Meduesa's
f
a
l
l
e
n

head,
or stoop,
and where the
golden c
u r
l
s with love
entwine,
the
serpents blood
sucked,
shall with
new life direct your
footsteps back across
theMELTINGEARTH.

|||
———————

Died: September 1960

Goodbye Apollo

Sad, that some dreams should disperse.
Lost perhaps with your going.

How can we bear this parting?

Us precious poets who've nursed you for so long,
who've seen in word and deed your glorious decline
know you have no home,
know, that like a disappearing shadow, you hurry
to be gone.
For it is long since suppliants came to Delphi,
Long since Sibyls sang your song.

Perhaps, in an ecstatic moment, some one of us
will feel your hand reach down and part the
centuries, feel you pass ghostlike through
the world, or see your flame, though flickering
dim, alight in a companion's eyes ---------- then,
extinguished and forgotten; die.

We've proved unequal to your golden charm,
and many before have passed your way,
to lay in the collective grave of
tired and tarnished gods.

He who pays the piper

He who pays the piper
Could reap a riper crop
By stopping to remember
That whoever calls
The piper's tune falls flat,
Unless the rat's consulted,
Not didactically insulted
By the forceful imposition
Of a tempo from
an unfamiliar tune.

Some ignore this simple law
And impose the final score,
Thus; risking war
And leaving poor,
Even he who pays the piper.

Sunday Lunchtime Stripper

When she gracefully entered
the crude public bar
of the pub known locally
as the Piss-Hole and Star,
I thought she'd arrived from
A far distant place,
where the girls were
angelic and fairer of face
than the ones who frequented
this beer-swilling den,
this drunken abode
of insensitive men.
I thought when I saw her
there's many a bar,
much nearer by far,
to the girl which you are,
than this loud crowd;
who drooling like dogs
thought you may be,
the perfect performer in
their sad fantasy.
Yet, when you appeared
As a stripper in chains,
You became the source
of my infinite pains.

Listen!

Now that AIDS, and frigid maids
and strident anti-men brigades
have fucked-up sex,

and money-crazed moguls
and mad-mullahs of hate
have fucked-up everything else.

Let's consign man's savage breed
to seed the cosmos with his dust.
And forever end
the unremitting pain
of his brief and evil reign.

We need to build and detonate
a hundred thousand million,
billion, trillion, trillion
megaton bomb.

And make a bang *so* big,
the space between the stars
would shiver with the shock.

And interrupt
the cosmic clock
just long enough
to mark our species
final end with a light
so bright, that night and us
shall cease to be,
and all eternity
will know our absence
as no more,
than filaments of failure
trailed between the stars.

Some idle thoughts on grass and stubble

I've got grass and I've got whiskers,
Both need cutting frequently,
And the older I become
The more that this depresses me.

Although my grass sometimes lies dormant,
Waiting for the sun to shine,
My whiskers, they just keep on growing,
Even though the day's not fine.

The other thing that's real annoying,
Is, that with some modest care,
My grass, just keeps on getting better,
It shows no sign of wear and tear.

And though I give them more attention,
Shaving stubble every day,
How do my facial hairs repay me?
By growing tough and turning grey.

It Was a Loneliness

It was a loneliness,
Yet incomplete,
Something of myself
I could not give.

No struggle?
No last plea?
No desperate
tear upon my inner
eye,

I

saw
you
Profoundly mouthing
your
Chang
ing im
age.

While

I stood silent,
ineffective;
and watched from   f a r   a   w   a   y
Myself destroy us.

Natural Disaster

An elegy to all the victims of this capricious world.

Words aren't enough, the common tongue
judged useless to expunge our deepest grief.
Yet what else have we?
Music perhaps, gestures, grunts, touches
of cold comfort?
Rage exhausts itself, searching vainly
for some culprit.

We return to words and find them wanting.
Trusting others to know enough
to know just how we feel.
Continuing to mouth our vain attempts
to tame the savagery of loss.

Words aren't enough we know.
We know, we know not what to say.
Yet speak and keep on speaking.
In the end; it's all we know.

Infinity

Infinity might be a lie.
Know; you and I shall cease to be
And all humanity eventually shall die.

That time and space
May race to singularity
Can give a freedom
Which eternity denies,
Winds chains of hope around
Our scope for action.

Cosmic reaction to the gravity
Of mass despair
Will make a solar flare
Seem small compared to ends
Which physics teach.
Though we could reach
A billion, billion years,
Still, human fears,
Banish tears enshrined
In finding reasons.

Sufficient seasons notice change,
Time for rearrangement of the wrong.
Prolong the outward song
Restructure stars
When farthest worlds are fried
Inside the sphere of solar death.
The breath of life can last,
But not surpass the final fate.
Which waits
Expansion or Collapse?

Perhaps we'll live as far
As light from farthest stars
Has yet to run.
Begun to know
How atoms grow
To complex double helix,
Mixing mind and space
In the same race,
To glean some meaning
From our cosmic place.

While some ask why
Let you and I
Sigh "Just as well."
Fulfil our now with
Simple shrines which
Minds like mine can comprehend.
Face the feeling all shall end
By sending song of this small race
To chase along the space
Between the stars.
And, confront the final days
With humble words of human praise,
To raise amazement;
Even from the gods.

Night in a Disco

I wonder why I'm here
when I can see so clearly,
how the time's miss-spent.

Some girls push past
with loves, which last
as long as music fast
keeps all joy jerking
puppet-wise to unseen ties,
and psychedelic lights
effect hallucinatory hues
infusing all.
In tune with sound
as round and round
they're twirled,
now red,
now white,
now green,
the scene all animation,
but expressions blank.

I sink a numbing drink,
thinking to edge despair
into some corner, where
the spare is of another kind,
where I can find a fellow
mind with body sweet,
and time to meet
the unexpected.

And though I know
fulfilment lies elsewhere,
a pair of lovely legs
begs for attention of a
different sort, where thought
is less important than intent,
and talking something for the old;

like me.

Nicotine Queen

For the gloriously addicted. May they always inspire us.

I'm one of life's serious smokers
Not one of your three-a-day jokers
Who claim they can quit whenever they choose,
Or, only light up when they're out on the booze.

Oh no! I'm a nicotine queen.
By my looks you may guess where I've been,
What pleasures I've had for being so bad
What joys I have missed by looking so sad.

Yet, please don't despair for my fate.
Or, imagine for me it's too late.
Don't judge me for looking a fright,
Just come here, and give me a light.

For, I am a nicotine queen,
Who's enjoyed the foul weed since a teen.
I'm one of life's serious smokers,
Not one of your three-a-day jokers.

November 5th 1980

For Sally

I journeyed to an unfamiliar place,
To frame your known and lovely face
Within the small yet feeling space
Between the fond intention of my hands.
And, had no plans for you to know
How time dilates the slowness of
Our separate days, where we both stay
Disguised, among the wrong established choice
Which younger voice; thought right.
Yet for tonight, you let me see
How it could be if others claim
To call your common name; were through.

Why then, should I feel blue
Now that at last, you've said,
"I love you too?"

Night Quatrains

We enter one another's dreams like mist
An insubstantial lost protagonist
Trailing stardust, touching ancient lips
Returning life to those once kissed.

Infusing sleep's nostalgic picture-show
With images of lovers long ago
We waken to a fading sense of loss
Like a twirled sparkler's after-glow.

On the Same Day

On the same day as a car,
Carrying man, wife and three children
Crossed the central reservation,
Your fingers, fragile as a butterfly
Compelled my flesh to life.
Moving us beyond specific endings;
While somewhere else, an unsuspecting wife,
Returned to find her husband hanged
Within the confines of a room
Where once, they had conceived a dream.

On the day, that you and I
Forgetful from each other's kiss
Let passion fuse our separate flesh,
Dispelling past and futures with each breath,
Five men inside an armoured car,
Who may have loved before,
Or, lived to taste oblivion again,
Were carefully partitioned by a bomb.

When we, as lovers, lay together,
Learning from each tender touch
The contours of desire,
A young boy, barbed by broken vows
Blew out his mind.
Bequeathing unto death
The final affirmation of despair.

As our liked bodies lived
The mutual length of ecstasy,
Excluding expectation and recall,
A sterile room, its starkness
Softened by cut flowers,
Was witness
To a mother's leaving kiss.

On the same day as my living seed
Erupted in your womb, to shrink
Perception of our universe to one
Sensation greater than this tiny room,
Many minds discovered space too large;
And found such moments as we shared,
Too rare a compensation for their loss.

Amuse Bouche

Opinions!

Opinions are nice when I own them,
When they're ones which belong first to me,
I like nothing more than to voice them
And stir up some controversy.

This is achieved very simply,
For instead of accepting I'm right,
Most people hold views contradictory,
Thus proving they're not very bright!

Places

Places; being only people,
can easily depress
if we compress all possibilities
to the here and now.

The hugest whole
might be nowhere
to house the soul.

Location is of mind,
where we can find
some kindred kind.
Although the spot be small
it's not at all the size
compels, we realise the
finite probability of find,
nor mind the many, who
we may not ever meet.
To be complete
some warm retreat
is most times self-sufficient,
to the why we went.

And though our finite fear
induces panic, that it is not here,
where love and life and destiny will meet,
another street, or different place,
perhaps provides the face,
but not the case for proving
that the moving of the scene
can mean serenity,
or something new discovered
of the world.

The possibilities have always
been of here and now.

Relationships Grow Wrinkles

Relationships grow wrinkles
far beyond the power of creams.
And care-worn skin grows paper-thin
beneath time's fleeting dreams.

We can't remove, or iron smooth
the lines which mark our life.
Or repair the love we share
beneath a surgeon's knife.

We should use gently what we value most
not crush the hopes of lovers.
For unlike skirts or rumpled shirts
we can't iron the hurt of others.

One of the Few

For a friend who enjoyed a
brief moment of fame

How is it, that you
Were one of the few
To shine through?
We'd shared the same past,
And some of us fast,
But most of us slow
Had nowhere to go;
Though you had arrived
While most of us lied,
And tried to pretend
We'd been a good friend
In the past.

You sported a name
Symbiotic with fame.
Is the price which you paid
What made us afraid?
Or, was morality yours
And ours the flaws,
Which make us recall
How the time we had bought

Just as dearly as you
Has all turned to naught?
Leaving tears to tarnish
Your stardust like rust.

The sad truth is that,
The dreams which we shared
Are with us all still,
And continue to kill,
By degrees.

Poem for my Godson

Because I had been asked
I came to pledge my care for you,
And stand in plain and profane sight
Of those who'd brought their frail beliefs
Into this sunless shrine.
Where divine protection, dearly bought,
Provided poor relief to ease the fierce grief
Which holiness employs
To bless the testing time
Your ripening years shall bring.

A superstition almost passed
Had cast perdition from frail minds.
Providing moments to forswear
Their love affair with Mammon's need
To feed all thoughts of sanctity into the
Greedy years, where new agnostic fears
Of failure taught that faith was naught
But baseless hope.

Knowing that reality beyond these
Hallowed walls, appals the call
Of mysteries, waking them
From shallow sleep to keep their dread
Of nothingness at bay.

Still, for today they summoned care,
To swear for you a Christian view,
Within which few can truly keep
The weeping needed to sustain
The pain which guilt exacts
From this first pact with God.

Poetry

A tribute to Dylan Thomas

The feeling's old
The language cold
The subject's small
The stories tall.

The wordsmith's world
contracts to catch
reflections of reality
upon a printed page.

Where is the rage?
New wave rejects
effects, where words
could fork "no lightning."

And cerebral verses
rise to arid skies,
where no "blue trades"
are practised now.

Circumspect and circumscribed
the current lines imbibed
no inspiration from
that grander cup,
where wines had liberated lines
Like, "Light breaks where no sun shines."

And most that cry
do so upon a shrinking stage,
their cage expression,
and their rage restricted
to a sterile play on words.

The form austere
The view unclear
The motive fear
The eye is dry.

Prayer

The dreams we keep in grown-up sleep
Bring nightly visions of a place
Where time and space
Have ceased to be.
A magic place,
Where we can be,
Free to choose
How lovers win and cynics lose.
Where night shall bring such
Soothing songs to right past deeds
And ancient wrongs,
Dispelling fears of demons past
Bringing perfect peace at last.

May all our dreams
from childhood come
nightly with the end of real,
And brightly burning, make us feel
As we did when we were young,
Reborn each morning with the sun.

Please put down that book

Please put down that book you're reading now,
And, gently close its pages
So no harm shall come
To damage its cold thought.

Look up. Please, look up and see
What little there is left of me
To resurrect the days where you felt loved.

Requiem for the Rhondda

Here, in these steep valleys
dreams were born.
Shorn of inherited illusion
I cast an Englishman's eye
upon this skyline of
dark hills and dying chimneys.
A place where trees, like men
Are stunted from fire's hunger
to consume both fuel and
feelings in time's subtle flames,
and the most wonderful women
on earth beckon a welcome
from worn doorsteps.
The need now,
is to understand how
women scrimped and scraped
whilst boys escaped,
to leave these valleys
raped of coal, to old men,
their faces full of forgetting,
and, to grieving girls
whose lilting voices and
lovely bodies weaved magic
between mountains and mountings.

In the shade of once green hills,
And tall towers of fruitful trees,
eaves of slate still cast familiar shadows
in narrow streets,
and something beats
which tames time's
relentless tick and fearful tock.
To see beauty here
requires a nearness, denied.
A growing, a knowing,
a sowing of seeds
with people not places.
To see in the faces
ancestral expressions
that transcend chapels,
and choirs and dragons
and rugby and leeks, but
speaks of these valleys
with authentic voices;
rejoicing a birth of belonging,
stranding strangers like me
on shores of loathing and longing.

How a conference speech was saved by a marvel of modern medicine

He left home that morning in terrible fear,
That his speech would be soiled by renewed diarrhoea
And that delegates waiting to savour his wit,
Would be all too aware of his great need to shit.

Yet he needn't have worried as he mounted the podium,
For he'd taken two capsules of trusty 'Imodium,'
So all of the delegates heard his wise words,
While the medicine worked to firm-up his turds.

Retirement

Without work, weeks wobble.
Leisure leaks from weekends
Infecting weekdays
With the laziness
Of Sunday's soporific hours.
So, when you ask
"What day is it today?"
I struggle to recall.
For I,
Like you,
Have forgotten too
The shape of days,
The contour of the hour,
The power of Friday to excite
And the dread
Of Monday's
Siren call to work.
Days become as one,
No tasks to give them form,
And each one born anew.
With absolutely nothing,
We must absolutely do.

River of Life

Under a setting sun,
Silver bellied fish lie,
Each sightless eye
Lifeless with rebuke.
Trapped in endless eddies
Of our urban filth
Their once quick scales
Are dark and drying.
Their black-humped backs
And flattened fins, fast held
Mid dying reeds
And swirling foam,
Foretell our end.
Below the weir,
Where a year ago
So many salmon leapt
The old mill-race
No trace of life abides.
The tides of failure fill the air,
The careless stench of death
Stills my laboured breath,
And stings my eyes
With fruitless tears.

As darkness nears
I yet may dream,
Of a pure and crystal stream,
To wash away the guilt.

Sales Meeting

You'd think,
To watch them posture
In the preposterous privacy
Of their prosperous scene,
That all meaning's been reduced
To who's produced the greatest gain,
Or, avoided interruption, by the
Challenging corruption of a
Real and feeling pain.
Yet; they remain.
The same, year after year
They reappear to swill stale beer
And hear how well their own
Poor padded cell's performed.
Be warned!
Their mouths move with a motion
Which circumscribes
All that the eye requires
To be inspired.
Yet, just one,
Alert attentive ear,
Can hear quite clearly,
How they're really mouthing
Madness.

How can a man,
Take this once, forever trip
With no questions on his lip
As to the reason why?

See it Through

Wichita Lineman is what they'd played,
And I'd stayed too late,
In hope that fate
had plans for you and I.
But, it was not to be,
For unlike me
your mind was occupied elsewhere.

To see how it can end
when all is penned,
When everything I have to say
is spent and blown away,
And all I've ever been
is lent – to you, and you, and you.

Then what to do?
But see it through.

And captivate true friends
with deeds which make amends
For what I've been,
Or what I am,
Or what I may become.

Reasons

Reasons like seasons are changeable,
And bend to fit the action's needs.
Reeds swayed by summer breeze
are often more substantial
than the whys we give to
those, who wish to know the
causes for the pauses in consistency.

On the death of Margaret Thatcher

How to tell the truth
when all conspire to twist
history to reflect the aspect
they themselves admire?
Acolytes will never tire
of worship, as those whose
frailties were exposed by her,
will never tire of hate.

Her greatness in the end,
will not depend on noble deeds.
But maybe, on the narcissistic needs
of those, who'd close whole chapters,
just to ensure the poor
shall have no story
worth the tale.

And as we praise her legacy,
raising eyes to heaven
in her name,
it's best to reflect,
that fame, like fortune,
is diminished by the taint
of time's corrosive touch,
and she who values selfishness
too much, will in the end,
be more despised, than prized.

Omniscience?

Some minor character in a TV Sunday play
was asked to pick a day, (just one mind you)
that he would wish to live through once again.

And, do you know what?
Even though he seemed quite sane
he could not think of one.

Yet, don't think this odd,
for even God (speaking on a late-night show)
was slow to answer.
And when He did, admitted that the question
had outwitted even Him.
"The past's been grim." He said.
Adding, that the question was an unfair test.
But that, if pressed, He guessed
the best was still to come.

Now

There's only now.
There's only ever, now.

Lines can linger long upon
The printed page,
Where rage exhausts itself,
Transmitting thought
Down centuries of change
Promising a life remembered
Or, a future,
Where we transcend time.

Tempting us to live a half-imagined past,
Or dwell among uncertain dreams
Of futures filled with desperate hope.

The truth is:
Now is where we live.
There is only now.
There is only ever, now.
Now is all that ever was,
All that is,
And all which shall become.

Nightmare

Struggling to surface from
sleep's deepest trench
I smell the stench of life's decay,
and desire the day's release
from night's clammy dreams.
My silent screams are only heard
by the hellish bird
which plucked the viscid eyeball
from my screaming skull
to leave me sightless,
desperate for a dawn
I'll never see.

Mansions of the Mind

I dwell in mansions of the mind,
where memories of life reside.
Here my thoughts can swiftly hide
and friends converse in sunlit bowers,
or stroll
through gardens full of flowers.

The sky above is azure blue,
but can display a darker hue
when I consign some evil bore
deep beneath a marble floor
to languish in a mental cell,
where at my pleasure,
they will face,
cruel torments
of abject disgrace.

Here too, in soaring halls of light,
bright laughter fills the quickening night,
where loyal staff, prepare a place
when I no longer wish to face
the boredom of the commonplace.

My interiors are blessed with stairs
which rise to bedrooms, where await
lovers keen to titillate,
and sooth my fevered brow.

But just for now, I've closed a door
and settled on the cushioned floor
of my favourite retreat,
where life and love and meaning meet.
where safe in my imagination
I can sup the mind's libation.

Mondays

Mondays!
Christ! I'm dying of a surfeit of
Mondays,
It's ridiculous regularity
reduces me to numbness.

Some bored bastard
should have banished it long
ago.

We require some trick
between waking and dying
to shake Mondays up,
or aid its declining.

Letter to my Mother

Mother,
My newborn child,
kindled shaped and
fired in your love,
is
steering me back,
through channels
of ungrateful
adolescence.
Past stormy days
of alternating mood.
Past days when
I, in vampire mode
devoured your love's
eternal patience,
or,
as an angel from
a Christmas play
all paper wings,
crept nearer for
the stroke of
loving hands
upon his neck,
back,
back.
To days when

memory is nothing,
but the knowledge
that once,
like mine,
your body stooped
to scoop a crying
infant to your breast.
And sang in all its
joy when tiny fingers
found your hair,

or

balled themselves to
rub the sleep from
eyes, the crying
'whys' of which,
you comforted.

For those years then,
where memories
are yours.
Thank you.

Amuse Bouche

Shoes

There are shoes
made for walking
and stalking
and running,
for prancing and dancing.
and smoothly romancing.
Shoes built for soccer,
or, cycling and hiking
for climbing and mourning,
or circus performing.
Shoes made for hire
or, fighting a fire.
But the shoes I admire
are those which inspire
the writing of verse
and sometimes, much worse.

The Saving Slaves

It does not have to be
that we must forfeit freedom.

The current change arranges
strange new landscapes
for contemplation by
the mind's dark caves.

Be sure!
The saving slaves will come,
bequeathing wild winds
to whistle through
the wandering thoughts
of newly idle men.

And this, can mark the when
that sees our reasons
bloom in room fresh found.
To find that mind
is more than just a store
for mundane pain
occasioned by the need
to feed the body's plea
to see the dawn again,
and tread the mill
that robs the will of strength
to fight the night which everywhere,
descends.

The end Greek freemen knew.

Few create the greatest gifts.
Production of the true
and polished curve of marble gods
required that the rods be used
on men abused by freedom,
to serve the talent and make time
to spend in epic rhyme.

For those whom fortune chose
to favour with the craft and art
to part the years -----------------
linking generations with the thought
so dearly bought in bondage.

They laid the prize
which opened later eyes,
and prompted 'whys'
which surface still
amid the spires
and learned domes
of academic stay-at-homes.

We have the chance
to rearrange the dance.
So that the wings
which let the poets soar
could be attached to more
than just the few
who threw good men away,
to wait the day when all should end.

It was an old hotel

It was an old hotel,
With clientele so well preserved
They'd all reserved a restaurant place
In tasteless cries of senile haste.

Perhaps, in case their
Goose was cooked
Before they'd booked a space,
Or, died before they'd tried
The pan-fried trout.

Company Reps

I guess we've all met the kind
who unwind at the bar
after travelling far.
Their journeys by car
are of time and of space,
but their faces reveal
that the distance they feel
is not one of miles;
It's rather the smiles
of separation from self
which light up their eyes
with 'whys' that inspire
a wish to enquire
Where are they from?
Where are they bound?
What have they found?

Could it be
that like me
they are lost?

Limits

Beyond the limit of what can be said,
Is this terrible pain in my heart.
In my head,
Move the words which I fashion
To carry the weight
Of a knowledge
They weren't built to bear.
They buckle and bend
Into cliché or worse,
As I try to make verse
Tell *all* that I know.

Beyond language
Lies a loneliness
Too profound for words.

A Meeting

What should we make of this?
This present which betrays us
As it moves.

What can we say?
If this brief meeting of
Our voices serves only
To illuminate some dark
And fleeting seconds with
A smile.

What can we do?
When yesterday
There was no you.

Must our future be
The half-remembered
Promise of a look?

A future where we have
Nothing,
But a memory, unrealised.

Like the after image of a
child's sparkler twirled in
darkness, we are cold and
disenchanted by a circled
light which dies upon
the air where it was born.

Holy Attire

A nun in the sun
was heard to declare
"I'm as hot as a bun
with a cross to bear."

Her companion replied
"And I'm really cooking.
I'd cast my habit aside,
but the Lord may be looking."

So they sat on the beach
and prayed for a breeze
to refreshingly reach
past their slightly spread knees.

New Year 2014

New hour, new day, New Year.
Dawning to the howl of wind.
Waking to the wails and tales
Of the newly dispossessed.
Arriving where religion rules,
Where fundamental fools
Decorate strange streets
With victim's severed limbs.
Flicking switches to extinguish
Lives much worthier than theirs.
So, welcome to the coming year
Where fear will stifle truth
And youthful eyes, still full of 'whys'
Continue to cry tears of blood.

Circle of Knowledge

As mysteries are removed
and science proved a bright
revealing light which pushes
back expanding blackness;
so too, do all but few observers
find they're caught within a thin
expanding ring of constant dusk.

On the border of two zones
they grow, but cannot bear
the brilliant glare of brightness
knowledge brings.

Nor does the cold
far older night of ignorance
embrace them with its touch.
They know too much
for such a sweet escape
to greet them with its
numbing chill.

Still, they're trapped in unmapped lands
between voids close to hand
and lights of bright despair
that there, they shall remain.
To sing their song of wished for fame,
and prepare their barren
stage for future pain.

Lamenting sunshine
squandered in their name.

Dare

Mountains may seem unscalable,
whilst you appear available.

Both suppositions may be frail
when it's just the fear of
failure which prevents events,
and 'wents' only remembered
as occasions that occurred.

From all I've heard
reality requires risk.

For death demands that,
a degree of dare be spare,
for living to be less a chore,
and more a rare affair.

Hedgehog

A hedgehog left its safe daylight abode.
Needing to traverse a care less road
That flowed its hard black strength
An unforgiving length across an ancient track
Which dated back to time before
A landscape scored with sudden light
Would frighten soft small squelchy things
With recent risks our swiftness brings.

This night,
Its last and fast as could go pace
Had proved too slow for it to win the race,
Or know, its nightly jaunts,
To seek old haunts; were past.

How Easily

How easily,
The irresponsibility
Immediacy requires,
Begins small fires.
Which turn to pyres
Before reality enquires
The cost.

Fundamentalism

Freedom's such a fragile gift,
Bought dearly with copious blood
Of guileless youth, too young by far
To fully comprehend
The irredeemable finality of death.

It's tragic when we know so much,
Can access with an on-screen touch
The truth of how we came to be
Yet, neither you, nor me, or anybody else,
Knows how to counter the insanity
Of a fundamental wish to subjugate us all.

How may we strive to win
This crazy contest for control?
Born from religion's dreadful dreams
To dominate the world.
How shall we reasonably explain
To our betrayed and unborn young
Our failure to confront this
Life denying vision of a world
Controlled by bigotry and fear?

How might we one day, finally persuade
Those who love death, to cast aside their
Terrifying certainty of faith,
And finally, embrace the freedom
Which can only come from doubt?

To W B Yeats

I know what Yeats meant
When he sent his soul ahead
To seek the rage that age commands.

The toll which was paid
In laid aside days
Allowed him the truth,
To see how spent youth, required
That tired observers depart.
To practice their art
In a partitioned cell,
Where the "Shall"
Of the young
Had too early become
The "Why?"
Of the dying.

Fort Hood Texas

November 2009

What good's intelligence
If it fails to inform the secret
Watchers of our deeds
How an ancient desert creed
Can convince a fertile mind
To find religious reasons
To extinguish life?

We must believe these
Haters of our lives
For they tell us every day
Our way must be destroyed.

What will it take, for us
Who love and value life,
To finally awake?

I Remember

I remember it rained
on the day we buried
Aunt Alice.

No malice implied
by the weather.
She'd died, we'd cried.

The mood of the day
had much more to say
of the way,
Than all the babble
in the Chapel of Rest.

Waiting

Tonight
I w a i t   for you.
Not with hope,
But expectation.

Though late
I WAIT.

And in the wait,
My dreams,
My doubts
and
Our dilemma
Delude me.

Do such delusions
make demands?

The clock takes no account
of the pauses between
heartbeat and heartbreak.

Dreams

The city sleeps now,
caged and tamed behind
my mind's most sensual schemes.
And here, where starlight
shines between the bars
of my desire, you wait.
Not looking at the lover's moon
or me,
but sensing with distracted eyes,
the fearsome ties, which
bind us to the joy to come,
and gives our fun some purpose
far beyond the trap I'd built to house
the sweet compliance of your lust.
I wake regretfully,
and all this promise turns to dust.
Far below the city's squalor waits
as cages open,
spilling onto stony streets
the remnants of
our scarce remembered dreams.

Arthurian Vision

Upon the farthest bank of legend's secret lake,
At the very edge of a summer day
The last long corridors of light, retract.
Bequeathing dusk his brief dominion
Over dreams and magic quests
And there, upon the mind's most distant shore
The ephemeral figure of an almost forgotten boy
Stood waiting for 'Excalibur' to rise.

To my wife on our move to a new home in the country

Have we now found Utopia, Shangri-La?
Call it what you will
It still,
Is just a state of mind
Where we will find
But what we make.

Take our new view
Of undulating pastures green
And of trees seen, and loved.

Horizons far and space to run;
Where fun, is rediscovered,
And the sun,
Whose cloud tossed light
Makes landscapes flow
With bright
And sometimes darker hues.

Will blues pursue us here?
Will fear,
Of what has been
Or what's to come
Continue to possess us?

For I doubt if the mere presence of a view
Can be the instrument to build our life anew,
And kinship with the earth
Means no rebirth
Of feeling dead or dying.

But as the sighing wind can welcome sunshine
Or betoken calm before the storm,
So can our love, both cool and warm
Find here a new beginning,
Or an end.

Final Silence

there are no birds,
or flowers,
or running
hand in hand.

hopeful eyes,
once mirrored
in imagined futures
reach their final view

parched lips,
upon whose
cracking flesh
wine flowed,
laughter bubbled,
and love pressed
his brief desire
now fade.

lined hands,
once moved with gestures
touched by dreams,
claw the winding shroud
with talons of despair

I care,
for everyone who
dies,
not knowing
where the time has gone,
or why.

we die
no closer to the truth,
yet having known the
intense fragility
of our ephemeral youth.

A Poem for My Wife

No 'work of words' for you.
Why such omission,
when you've meant more
than all of those
who've gone before?

I guess, because with you
I've felt no sense of loss.
No reason to disperse my fear
of loneliness with words.
Or need to harness your belief in me
by fixing pain upon a printed page.

Edward Woodward's Dream

Edward Woodward had a dream
Which forced from him a fearful scream,
For in his dream a demon came
To steal the 'd's' out of his name.

So vivid was this bad nightmare,
That Edward now has lost his hair,
But worse than this, much worse by far,
Is now he's called, 'Ewar Woowar!'

Staid

Show me the way,
the action's stayed
here in a groove,
and hard to move
I find familiar fare
the easiest to bear.

Some reason I require
to relight a fire
which burned so brightly
long ago,
know, that all paradise
in bloom must soon
make room for us,
the disenchanted.

The Game

It's regrettable,
but unforgettable
how female forms
flatter the fickle.

What's the matter
is that skilful patter
can only satisfy the frame.

That game at least is understood.

The name, however,
requires much,
that such small talk
cannot fulfil,
Or ever has,
Nor ever will.

The Sum

The fastness of the moment
seemed locked tight.
And might have proved eternal
had the light not failed.

I sailed, and all the earth
was rounder than a sphere.
Nowhere is here
50,000 pints of beer
And one life, gone.

Remember all.

The song's not wasted,
the wine is tasted,
the lips are kissed,
and though some are missed
the sum of all is this:

LIFE = SIGNIFICANCE – DEATH > 0

Amuse Bouche

"Easy"

_____

She had a nice neat arse,
But like a farce the label
on her blue and straight
legged jeans read

"Easy".

And like the proffer
of some special offer
I knew the label lied,
'cause when I tried;
She sighed;

And turned me down.

The Grim Reaper

If you must come, as come you must,
Don't come in winter and awake
The fat cat dozing by the fire.
And don't appear in fertile spring
When birds begin to sing of love
Above new shoots of verdant grass.
Summer's not the time to call
And is the least good time of all,
When nights are light, and loved ones
Bright with hope, can't cope with death.
Autumn might just be OK,
Unless I'm feeling fine and well
Then it would be capricious
And suspicious if you call
When all of life's still full of fun.
So, when all is said, and all is done,
Perhaps it's best you do not come,
At least for many seasons still,
Until my will to live is gone
And I can welcome you with song.

Moments

On days possessed by moments
still enough to foster thought,
I'm reminded, just how dearly bought
is all the business which stifles grief.

Amuse Bouche

Men and Multi-Tasking

Those claiming men can't multi-task
Should ask themselves, can this be true?
For clearly, when there's much to do
Some guys can drink and talk and woo
And listen as they lick and screw.
Thus proving, when the tasks are fun,
It's easy to do more than one.

Humanity

Humanity, whom I have never loved
Can leave me with dismay
At its array of triviality.

Normality is hard to bear
When I'm aware
That sometime,
Somehow and perhaps somewhere;
But more especially someone
Can make the fun,
Provide the light,
That makes the sunshine bright
The night more right,
And gives the fight to live
An edge that's often blunted
By the boredom of the birth
Of ordinary days.

It's not just praise that satisfies,
Who provides the prize should realise
That what's required
Is not retired minds
Where finds are difficult to make.

I need a risk like gamblers take
Where the rake-off could be high enough
to make the sky seem small.
So that even when compared
With all that is or's ever been
The momentary scene could shrink
the total cosmos to a single wink,
and encompass in an eyelids twitch
The which,
The how,
The when,
The why.

So that
Just once before I die,
The reason for the pain
Is plain.

The Gulls

Beyond this stormy shore
gulls soar, zagged and buffeted.
Modifying flight, they flip from grey
to white and light the day
with sudden and sustaining flare of wing.
They fling their competent contempt
into cyclonic air's attempt
to tear them from the sky.
And brilliantly defy the ancient try
of conquered gales to dash their
frailty into the sounding spray,
which spumes tall fumes of mist
to kiss their skill.

Speech Trap

Something spoken,
a truth revealed
has rung a bell
within the sound
of which, we must
henceforth
forever dwell.

My Need to Tell

"My language is the universal
whore whom I have to make into
a virgin"
Karl Kraus

My need to tell translates my thoughts
To words which have been tarnished
By the constant touch of many voices.
Leaving my language tainted by the
Coarseness of Plebeian lips.
Words are my tools in need of transformation,
My task to buff them so they shine like new.
Bringing to my work, a truth
Beyond the reach of common tongues.

We Cast Pale Shadows

We cast pale shadows after death.
Not as before,
A black and changing silhouette
Etched on a solid surface
By the sun.
Or, diffused by friendly light
Within familiar rooms.

We become as sudden air across
A candle flame,
Ephemeral as a single breath,
Rare as rainbows on a
Cloudless day.
Disturbing none, but those who
Loved us, for so brief a time.